ERGIS MECAJ

Our Sun,

Earth,

and Moon

Poems

Order this book online at www.trafford.com
or email orders@trafford.com

Most Trafford titles are also available at major online book retailers.

Printed in Victoria, BC, Canada.

ISBN: 978-1-4269-2333-3

Library of Congress Control Number: 2009913680

*Our mission is to efficiently provide the world's finest, most comprehensive book publishing
service, enabling every author to experience success. To find out how to publish your book, your
way, and have it available worldwide, visit us online at www.trafford.com*

Trafford rev. 12/15/2009

 www.trafford.com

North America & international
toll-free: 1 888 232 4444 (USA & Canada)
phone: 250 383 6864 ♦ fax: 812 355 4082

To my mom, my dad, my friends, and my other inspirations.

-E.M.

Table of Contents

All in a Day

I wake up when the sun will rise.
I brush my teeth; I wash my eyes.
I get dressed and breakfast I eat.
I wait for the bus down the street.
I leave to school; I learn and know.
On the school bus then I go.
I eat my lunch; I watch TV.
Then my homework I must see.
I eat my dinner without a peep.
I get out of my clothes and I sleep.
I am done until tomorrow.
It's all in a day, without any sorrow.

My Mind

My mind is a wonderful thing, you see,
And I'm not talking about the brain.
It's really just a part of me.
I have fun without any pain.

My imagination has no limit.
Think of all the possibilities.
I have my own world in it,
Without any possible boundaries.

In my mind, I've got knights
Battling some kings.
After a few crazy fights
I can change some things.

I change my whole entire mind
And make a future city.
Hovercrafts are what you'll find
And robots, none a pity.

As you see, my mind's a tool
For unlimited fun.
I hope you thought that it's real cool,
But my poem is done.

Birthdays

Birthdays are fun.
You feel number one.
You turn a year older.
You feel stronger and bolder.
On this day you'll feel pleasant.
You'll receive birthday presents.
You may act suspicious.
The cake is delicious.
Open gifts, what a surprise!
You can't believe your eyes.
This birthday was nice.
I wish it came twice!

My Parents

My mom and my dad are the best parents ever.

They nurture me dearly, and they both are so clever.

When I am depressed, they're right by my side.

When I have a secret, with them I'll confide.

They make all my meals; they dress me and adorn.

Without them together, I'd never have been born.

They support me and comfort me, like a family tree.

If a guy would trade for them, I'd never agree.

My mom and my dad are the best in the Earth.

They're priceless, but love me, and their love is their worth.

Your Room

There's a little place that I know.
If you want to find out, here's where you go:
To your room, 'cause your room is the best it can be.
When you're in your room, you always feel free.
It's where you can cry, making your eyes all wet.
It's where you have fun, moments you won't forget.
Your room may be private; it is just for you.
You can read a book; have an adventure, too.
You can do your homework; gather your knowledge.
Rooms even vary to dorms in a college.
Also, your bedroom is where you can rest.
So, in conclusion, your room is the best!

Someone

Someone right here is alive today.
Someone will work and someone will play.
Someone will sleep and wake up each day,
If it's sunny or if it will rain.

Someone will ask, "Who, where, and why?"
Someone will laugh and someone will cry.
Someone will achieve their goals if they try,
If they don't, they try again.

This someone is someone you've already seen.
Maybe it's happy; maybe it's mean.
If you want him to train you, don't be jealous and green.
It's you, so you don't have to train.

Us Heroes

For some people, the meaning of "hero"
Is someone courageous with weaknesses zero.
But you don't have to come from another planet.
You don't have to be strong and break granite.
You don't have to fly fast all around.
You don't have to run at the speed of sound.
All you need is you yourself.
You'll put villains on the shelf.
There are lots of people you can rescue.
I just have one thing to ask you:
Do you have to fly in the air
For people to adore you everywhere?

Walking Down the Street

When you walk down the street,
There are people that you meet.
Every friend you see
Knows your identity.
If you're going to grocery shop
At the store, you always stop
To talk with family and friends
Until the conversation ends.
There are always folks you see
By the store or library.
You seem to stop and talk
Before you go and walk.

Poetry

Poetry's
A passion, see,
How all the words
Are controlled by me.

I scribble the page
With fury and rage,
Trying to open a poem
Like curtains on a stage.

An idea spark
Comes out of the dark
And talks really loud
Like a little dog's bark.

And when I'm completed,
My poem is greeted,
I start to imagine
One more poem while I'm seated.

Poem's Process

Poetry unleashes spirit.
In your mind you'll almost hear it.
Thoughts will start a poem's birth.
You'll make a poem down-to-earth.
You just start with one small verse.
It grows and grows until it'll burst.
Sheets get filled with words of wonder.
Lyrics and rhymes from deep down under.
Joy and bliss and having fun.
You'll work hard until you're done.

Poet's Block

I tried to write a poem, see,
But no words came to my mind.
I tried and tried to think one up,
But inspiration I couldn't find.

I started to look all around me
And photographs came in my brain.
Then I really got to brainstorm.
I heard the thunder and the rain.

Finally, I wrote a poem.
Guess which one I wrote that day?
If you guessed that I wrote this one,
You're right! What do you have to say?

Spell "Poetry"

Passionate and optimistic.

Our ideas realistic.

Every word jumps on the page.

Truly skilled, scribbling with rage.

Relax your mind, and take it slow.

You finished a poem! Way to go!

Growing Stories

An empty page sits upon you.

You can control what it can do.

The pencil hits the sheet very tough.

A letter forms, but that's not enough.

More letters are written, forming a line.

Words are created, if they combine.

Words come together to develop a sentence.

Then comes a paragraph, each word an apprentice.

Pages and pages get filled with thought.

You've made a story that began from a dot.

Little Paper

It's white, it's blank, and it's made of tree.

It's all a writer needs to see.

With a pen gripped tight in hand,

He fills it with a language land.

Varieties from A-Z,

The ink dances happily.

It all starts from the cranium.

Out it pops like a geranium.

The paper's now home to fun.

Every letter joins as one.

Now, the paper lives in glory

As a page inside a story.

Haiku x2

Poems come from heart.
Not just what the brain thinks up,
But emotions too.

Here's one way to show
How your feelings come in words.
It's called a haiku.

The Night Shift

When I'm in my bed at night,
As I turn on my flashlight,
I have to write a poem, fast,
Or else my poem streak won't last.
Time to fire up my process.
Sometimes I have idea losses,
But in the end, I do fine.
That's how I wrote this poem of mine.

Our Sun and Moon

When I stare upon the sky,
Wondering what's impending,
The sun above just grabs my eye,
Knowing today's not ending.

We kids usually go to school,
And go outside and play.
But when the sun and ground must meet,
Together they'll end the day.

A million twinkles pass the sky,
A moon floats on the night.
We people tuck our beds tonight,
And sleep with covers tight.

Halfway across the globe,
Their timing's not the same.
When we're out, they're fast asleep,
When we snooze, they play their game.

Our Earth rotates around the sun,
The moon is orbiting us.
As day and night go in and out,
We people don't even fuss.

Light

If you want to improve your sight,

There's one thing you need: light.

Light has the most rapid speed.

Sometimes the sun is all you need.

With it, you can see all around.

Even light travels faster than sound.

The sun may help our sight in the day,

But at night, electricity lights our way.

Light bulbs candles, whatever it can be,

Light is the key source to how we see.

Without light, I couldn't write this poem.

These are light facts; now you know them.

The Sun and I

I look up as I'm walking by.
I take a good stare at the sky.
Then the sun just smiles at me.
Its rays come and tickle me
Like little fingers, big and bright.
It warms me with its cozy light.
I smile back and say, "Hello.
I'm very sorry. I must go
Back home." Next, the sun did say,
"I'll be waiting here next day."

Lake Sunset

I stare on my balcony,
And what do I see?
A calm blue lake
As big as the sea.

The shimmering waters
Give a glimpse in my eye
As I see the sun setting
As it leaves the sky.

This soothing experience
I cannot believe
When I stare at the water
My eyes are deceived.

As the night rolls in,
The lake fades to black.
But I do not worry,
Cause I'll know I'll be back.

Night

When the sun is up and shining,
I go out to play.
But every day it seems to set
And therefore ends the day.

Then a rainbow covers the sky,
As beautiful as it can be.
Next it starts to get real dark;
So dark, you can't see.

But after that the most beautiful
Thing starts to occur.
Silver stars twinkle in the shade.
The brightness makes it blur.

As I stare out my window,
I say, "What a sight to see!"
I wonder how day and night
Could act so differently.

Stars

The universe is home to lots
Of stars, which to us look like spots.
Stars are extraordinarily bright.
Stare up close and you'll lose your sight.
The sun we only see in the day.
Other stars are miles away.
Galaxies are made of stars.
They look like fireflies in jars.
So, next time you're out at dark,
Stare up and you'll see a spark.

Sleep

Every night I stare outside
My window into black.
I lay upon my cozy bed
For sleep is what I lack.

I close my eyes, signaling rest
As peace comes to my mind.
I put tomorrow in my sight,
And leave today behind.

I enter into worlds of black,
As my mind empties out.
Suddenly dreams start to form,
With colors all about.

Different nights have different dreams,
Some horror and some fine.
The fun ones make you want them more.
The nightmares tingle your spine.

At last, the sun wakes from its sleep,
And oddly, so do you.
Your relaxation's gone today,
But this night's surely new.

Earth

In the empty void of space,
Earth stands right in its own place.
The Earth has air sheets all around.
Gravity keeps our soil bound.
Water, heat, and vegetation
Help us live in our foundation.
Earth is home to many styles
Of animals within Sun's miles.
The Sun is home to many globes,
Circling it like little probes,
But Earth's the one that achieved much.
We're so glad it's in our clutch.

Seasonal Art

Every season, plants change color.
One season waiting after another,
It makes great art just like a painting,
Each different picture keeps on waiting.

In the springtime, all the trees
Turn a very bright shade of green,
Then comes out the warming sun,
And now it's time to start the fun!

When leaves turn dark green, then it's summer.
Here there's no need for a bummer.
The warming sun soon turns hot,
And staying warm is what you've got!

When it turns chilly, then it's fall.
Rolling in leaves and playing football.
The leaves soon fall, in shades of red,
Yellow, orange, brown, making a comfy bed.

In winter, there's a lot of snow.
Going outside is where some go.
Now all of the trees are bare,
Waiting for spring and leaves to wear.

The season cycle goes 'round and 'round,
Going on from town to town.
Winter, spring, summer, fall,
We love these seasons, we love them all.

Seasons

There are four parts to a year.
Each one spends its time right here.

Summer is a summer's breeze.
It rustles all the leaves and trees.

Fall makes leaves go everywhere:
On the ground and in your hair.

Winter is the coldest season.
When it's chilly, there's a reason.

When it's spring, you'll know soon.
The plants and flowers start to bloom.

Summer, fall, winter, spring,
Seasons are a beautiful thing.

Water

Water is a major source.
It guides us on the living course.
It gives support; it will endorse
Our being here today.

It quenches up our giant thirst.
Of other liquids, it comes first.
From lakes or ponds or a geyser's burst,
Or oceans by the bay.

Water now is very vital.
It's just like a worldwide idol.
Blue or clear (and this is final),
Water's great every way.

Flower's Life

It starts out as a little seed.
Light and water's all it need.
It starts to grow and then takes root.
Then pops out a little shoot.
The stem starts growing more and more.
The roots have spread out on the floor.
Leaves transform in many directions.
It catches up the sun's reflections.
Food is made and moved by stem,
Making this plant like a gem.
Water falls on leaves by drop.
A bud starts growing on the top.
Then it blooms into a flower.
It has bee-attracting power.
In the autumn, flowers die.
Cold comes as clouds fill the sky.
The pod opens as seeds come out.
They get spread all about.
Spring 'til fall, a flower's time
Ends 'til new ones come in line.

Weather

As the rain pours down,
As the snow drifts by,
As the sun beats down,
As the hailstones fly,

As tornadoes strike,
As hurricanes form,
As the wind blows hard,
Bringing with it a storm.

Do you think it's getting worse?
Do you think it's getting better?
No matter where you are,
It's all about weather.

Rain

Today is a rainy day.
I cannot go outside and play.
Instead I stay inside my house.
So does my dog, my cat, and mouse.

I watch the raindrops drop on the ground.
I hear a *dripping-dropping* sound.
Sometimes it's soft, like a drizzle,
Sometimes it's so hard it makes your hair frizzle.

Inside my house I read a book,
Or do a puzzle, or I'll look
Out my window just to see
Raindrops beating down on me.

Soon the raindrops start to soften.
Now they aren't beating down so often.
But still the rain keeps on pouring,
But now the rain isn't so boring.

Look! Look! The rain has ceased.
Now it's heading to the east.
I put on my hat, my boots, and coat,
And then I grab my red toy boat.

I say to mom, "I'm out for the day!"

And then I go outside to play.

But as I start to leave the den,

I wish for the rain to come again.

Storm

I'm watching weather on TV,
And see a storm's coming at me.
Dad comes home, tired and wet.
He's been out in the rain, I bet.
I see a quick flash in the sky,
And then I start to wonder why.
After that I hear a boom,
And I start running from the living room.
I look out my window and watch the storm,
Thankful that I'm staying warm.

Thank Goodness Santa Claus Could Swim

One day Santa Claus was fishing in the lake,
He didn't know a fish was coming at stake.
He felt a bite; he tried to reel it in.
He fell in the lake, but thank goodness he could swim.

    Thank goodness Santa Claus could swim.
    Thank goodness Santa Claus could swim!

He swam to shore; he saw his bite.
It caught his rod; it swam out of sight.
He tried to catch it, he fell again,
But thank goodness he could swim as fast as he can.

    Thank goodness Santa Claus could swim as fast as he can.
    Thank goodness Santa Claus could swim as fast as he can!

He went back home, sneezing like crazy.
When he came home, he felt so lazy.
When Mrs. Claus saw him, he made her eyes bolt.
"Goodness! You're sneezing! And you're allergic to salt.
Did you fish in The Great Salt Lake?"
"Yes," said Santa, "I made a mistake."
"Well," she said, "I'm glad you're in,
And I'm glad thank goodness you could swim."

    Thank goodness Santa Claus could swim.
    Thank goodness Santa Claus could swim!

My Bike

I ride my bike everyday.
When I ride, I go, "Whoowie!"
But my ride just ends up worse
Because I crashed into a tree.

I get up; I get back on my bike,
And pedal, pedal, and pedal.
But then I fell in a pile of leaves,
I guess I won't win the medal.

I have one more try; I get on my bike,
I fell into a den,
I broke my bone; I got a cast,
And I'm waiting to ride again.

A Green Fish

One day I want fishing
With Dad to catch some flounder.
We didn't catch a fish yet,
But other things I found there:
A rare coin, a clothespin,
A multicolored ball,
And the multicolored ball
Could even bounce off the wall.
But then I caught something extraordinary:
A light green colored fish,
And that light green colored fish
Was my very best wish.
I pulled and pulled; it tugged and tugged.
It tugged so hard I fell.
I got all wet and the fish swam away,
The fish I was going to smell.
So, at the end, the catch of the day
Wasn't my very best wish,
But at least we'll have to eat
Broccoli for our dish.

Normal or Not

Most people say to themselves,
"Today's a normal day."
But when I get out of my bed,
The opposite I say.
I brush my teeth with moldy sticks.
I eat my eyeball stew.
I slip on my snowman suit
And hop on top a gnu.
A jaguar chased me straight to school.
My homework ate itself.
My teacher likes to eat her feet,
And my best friend's an elf.
Art turned out to be "cancelled",
Gym class was "delayed".
In music my flute was swapped with
A jar of lemonade.
Today's lunch was roasted lion.
Recess wasn't fun.
The baseball was a rabid squirrel,
And someone stole the sun.
I ate my backpack as some dinner,
And slept on a porcupine.
Luckily, I was just dreaming.
Now where's that zebra of mine?

Reversible Writing

I'm writing this poem in reverse.
I have no reason why.
I hope you have a handy mirror
To read this with your eye.

Every time I try to write this
Normal, it won't work.
If I have to keep on writing,
I will go berserk.

I have tried some weird solutions
To fix this oversight
But every thing that I have tried
Just doesn't make it right

So, I had to give up somehow.
I can't switch it back.
Hey, at least this poem's title
Is on the right track!

Beach Fun

When you're at the beach, it's really fun,

Basking in the summer sun.

Build sandcastles to the sky,

Or strike a beach ball; make it fly,

Take a small stroll by the shore,

And you'll find crabs and shells galore.

Run to the water; take a swim.

Splash until the sky gets dim.

Today at the beach I had so much fun.

I'm so sad that the day is done.

Mystery Sleuths

Come on kids; let's solve a mystery.

We'll use facts and we'll use history.

In a mystery, there's suspense.

Gather the gang and let's commence.

We need to look for who did the crime.

Cracking this case won't take much time.

We'll get spooked; we'll get a scare.

Keep your eyes out; be aware.

We found the thief! The case is solved!

I'm so glad I was involved.

Food

In the morning or at night,
Hunger is never far from sight.
To satisfy your starving belly,
Go to the kitchen, bakery, or deli.
Either breakfast, lunch, or dinner,
Yummy food's always a winner.
Even snacks can't go wrong.
Culinary is going strong!
Dating back to the past,
Food is never always last.
So next time you want a treat,
Remember this: Food is neat!

Banana

Soft, squishy,
It's fun to eat.
A peel outside,
But inside it's sweet.
This yellow sensation
Is grown in the heat.
For some kids,
It's a yummy treat.
Due to other fruit,
It can't be beat.
You see these in markets,
Their peel's on the street.
Who am I?

Pizza

Welcome to my place.
Making pizza is so fun!
We'll put all the toppings,
One by one.

First we'll take the dough, and
Then we'll roll it out.
Then tomato sauce is
What it's all about!

Then we'll add some mountains
Of mozzarella cheese.
Then we'll add some cheddar and
Pepperoni, if you please.

Then we'll add some onions,
I will not make you cry.
Then we'll add some peppers,
Me, oh, my!

Then some Italian sausage,
Then we'll let it bake,
Then we're going to cut it,
Cut it like a cake.

Then we're going to eat it,
It's very delicious.
And with all our toppings,
It's also nutritious.

Thanks for helping me.
Making pizza is so fun!
But I'm very sorry,
Because now we're done.

Pets

Late one night I tried to ask
My mom and dad for dinner,
"Can I please have a pet?
I don't care if it's short or thinner.
I wonder if I had a dog.
It'll probably lick my face.
But what if we owned a cat?"
"It'll scratch all over the place."
"I think I'd like a pet parrot."
"But it shrieks and screams."
"It'll be cool if I had a ferret."
They said, *"In your dreams!"*
"What about a little goldfish?"
"I don't think you're ready."
"Think about a little turtle."
"It walks slow and steady."
After that, I begged and pleaded.
They said, *"We'll see."*
Now I care for a pet rock.
Wow, lucky me!

Piku

(Pee-koo)

I have this little cat,
Piku is its name.
I call and call; he runs away,
Thinking it's a game.

Piku, see, isn't a cat
Who stays inside a home.
He likes to stay outside all day
In shadows where he'll roam.

Piku's back is black and brown.
The rest of him is white.
He stays alert and looks around
With eyes so twinkling bright.

When I am far away from him,
He cries and cries a lot.
The two of us are best of friends.
I'm happy him I've got.

Travel

One rainy day I stood
Bored in my room.
I see lightning flashing
And hear thunder boom.

And as I see rain hitting
Hard on the gravel,
I started to wonder
How'd it feel to travel.

I'd be leaving my city,
I'd be leaving my state.
I'd be leaving my country,
And I would feel great.

I'd fly my big airplane
Over the ocean.
I'd see brand new lands
In one swift motion.

I'd see the Eiffel Tower
In Paris, France.
I would go to Spain
And learn how they dance.

Then I'd go to Egypt
And ride down the Nile.
It'll lead to the Amazon.
I'll see crocodiles.

I'd go visit China.
I'd go to Japan.
I'd go to Australia,
And more if I can.

I'd climb old Mt. Everest,
Tallest peak in the globe.
I'd even visit Mars
In a little space probe.

Yes, I'd go to these places,
And much and much more.
I would, but I can't even
Get out the door.

School

For some kids, it's a daily routine.
Some are for toddlers; some are for teens.
Get education while having some fun,
Dozens of subjects all fit into one.
Math, gym, art, and writing,
Art, music, isn't this exciting?
Science, reading, also social studies,
Lunch, recess, and hanging with buddies.
Classmates, teacher, the principal too,
The lessons, the classes, and don't forget you.
It's here all the time, except summer vacation.
School is a place to get education!

The Library

The library is a place that you can go
To figure out what you need to know.
With all the types of books and stories
Sorted into different categories.
Non-fiction, fiction, fantasy and mystery,
Science, biography, poetry and history.
Here there's any kind of book,
So come on down and take a look.
Here there are not only books you can see,
But also magazines, movies, videos, and DVDs!
So come on down to the library and take a look.
Now, if you'll excuse me, I'll go read my book!

Feelings

Everyday I seem to have ups,
And also I seem to have downs.
Sometime each day I carry a smile
And sometimes I'm wearing a frown.

It matters about the mood I am in,
It's the reason why I react.
When I am cheerful, tense, or annoyed,
My feelings control how I act.

When I'm excited, I jump up and down.
When I smile, that means that I'm glad.
When I'm upset, I put on a frown.
When I scowl, that means I'm real mad.

When I'm stressed out, I give a big sigh.
When I sleep, that means I'm worn-out.
When I'm depressed, I somewhat will cry,
When I'm scared, I scream and I shout.

So those are my feelings, moods, and my tempers.
I named a few inside and out.
Wait! There's one more that I feel about finishing:
When I'm proud, I stand without pout.

The Two Sides

When you see me face-to-face,
You only see just one.
But actually there're two of me,
One evil and one fun.

The nice me is as bright as sun,
As happy as a cat.
I'm swifter than cheetah's run,
As graceful as a bat.

I'm just as wise as an owl,
I stick to friends like paste.
I'm as sweet as apple pie,
Sweeter than its taste.

The evil me's a raging bull,
I'm as red as a cherry.
I'm as dirty as a dump,
Like a monster, I'm scary.

A dog isn't as bad as me,
I'm sneakier than snakes,
I'm as slippery as a fish,
I'm as hard as rakes.

So you've seen the real nice side,
You've also seen me mean.
I'll just ask you one more thing:
Which one would you've not seen?

Hope

When you're tense and
Stress comes along,
Do not fret,
Just be strong.
Hope will come and
Find its way,
Through the hassle
Storm that day.
Do not worry,
Just calm down.
Put on a smile
Instead of a frown.
Happiness and joy
May be gone,
But hope survives
And will move on.

Stress Reliever

When I'm stressed, when I'm tense,
When I don't know what to do,
When I'm feeling really mad,
Or when I'm feeling blue,

I don't puff, I don't stomp,
I just go to home,
I run to my balcony,
And my mind starts to roam.

The lake's waves are calming,
The clouds pass through the sky,
The sunsets are so peaceful,
The graceful birds, they fly.

Then I feel much better,
And my mind starts to clear.
And I'll say, "I am very glad
That I'm not stressed out here."

Green

Green is minty; green is lush.

Green is cabbage, and it's mush.

Green is shiny, like an emerald.

Green is lovely, also memorable.

Green is grass; green is leaves.

Green is broccoli, and lots of peas.

Green is frogs; green is lizards,

Sometimes green disappears in blizzards.

The top of a carrot is also green.

Green is happy; it's never mean.

Green is lettuce; green is mint,

Even the seawater has a greenish tint.

Green is snakes; green is moss.

Green is the color of the tie of a boss.

Green is a chalkboard; some crayons are green.

Green is seaweed, and a green bean.

Green is apples; Granny Smiths.

Green is the rainforest, and Christmas gifts.

Green is also a Christmas tree.

When we get presents, we shout with glee.

Green, to me, is the best color.

I like it more than any other!

Shadow

I have this twin brother when
I have no siblings at all.
At noon he's really tiny.
At sunset he's really tall.

He likes to be a copycat,
Copying my every move.
He sits when I sit,
He grooves when I groove.

Sometimes he likes to be a giant.
Sometimes he likes to be small.
But when I go to sleep,
I never see him at all.

Answer It

For every single situation,
There's always an explanation.
Find it; reach your destination.
You will have a reply.

Sometimes answers will be perfected,
Although some answers aren't corrected.
But whatever response you've connected
At least you gave it a try.

Musical Moves

You hear this funky music playing.
You really like the beat.
You just can't stop feeling the rhythm.
It makes you move your feet.

It doesn't matter what type
Of music it can be.
Just start playing you favorite tune
And after that, you'll feel free.

Bedtime's Poem

I'm sorry that this must end
For mom and dad, child and friend.
But every man must now just lie,
While the moon sings its lullaby.
I stare at the stars one more time.
Today I repose with no more rhyme.

Printed in the United States
by Baker & Taylor Publisher Services